Wisdom of the
African World

Wisdom of the African World

Selected and with
an Introduction
by
REGINALD MCKNIGHT

THE CLASSIC WISDOM COLLECTION
NEW WORLD LIBRARY
NOVATO, CALIFORNIA

The Classic Wisdom Collection
Published by New World Library
14 Pamaron Way, Novato, CA 94949

© 1996 Reginald McKnight

Cover design: Greg Wittrock
Cover illustration: Greg Wittrock
Text design: Nancy Benedict
Typography: Linda Corwin

Library of Congress Cataloging-in-Publication Data

Wisdom of the African world /
edited by Reginald McKnight.
p.   cm.   — (The classic wisdom collection)
Includes bibliographical references (p.) and index.
ISBN 1-880032-56-2 (alk. paper)
1. Quotations. 2. Quotations, English.
3. Blacks — Quotations.
I. McKnight, Reginald, 1956- . II. Series.
PN6081.3.W496 1996
081'.08996—dc20   95-38600
                                                          CIP

Printed in the U.S.A. on acid-free paper
Distributed by Publishers Group West
10 9 8 7 6 5 4 3 2 1

To Ludie P. Wooly

Acknowledgments

My thanks to Marc Levine, Angelique Hebert, and Michael Honch for all your help and advice. And a special thanks to Nora J. Bellows for your enthusiasm, advice, and impeccable eye for the quotable.

Contents

Publisher's Preface

Life is an endless cycle of change. We and our world will never remain the same.

Every generation has difficulty relating to the previous generation; even the language changes. The child speaks a different language than the parent.

It seems almost miraculous, then, that certain voices, certain books, are able to speak not only to one, but to many generations beyond them. The plays and poems of William Shakespeare are still relevant today — still capable of giving us goose bumps, still entertaining, disturbing, and profound. Shakespeare is the writer who, in the English language, defines the word *classic*.

There are many other writers and thinkers who, for a great many reasons, can be considered classic, for they withstand the test of time. We want to present the best of them to you in the New World Library Classic Wisdom Collection.

Even though these writers and thinkers may have lived many years ago, they are still relevant and important in today's world for the enduring words of wisdom they created, words that should forever be kept in print.

Wisdom of the African World is a very special book in this collection. It is, at various times, profound, enlightened, touching, poetic, and inspired. Every citizen of the planet Earth can gain value from the words and insights contained between these covers.

Marc Allen
New World Library

Introduction

Before I even began researching this book, I
knew it was going to be difficult to put together.
In the general sense, an editor of this sort of book
wants to be careful to maintain a reasonable
balance of the elements that hold it together.
There is the danger of including too many
Americans, or too few women, too many Nigeri-
ans, too few Senegalese. But try as one might,
there will be imbalances, for the compiling of
wisdom is an imperfect, ungainly art. Moreover,
I have found it particularly difficult to gather
these wise words under the rubric of "Pan-
Africanism" or "Africanity" or anything including the appellation "Africa," for the closer one's
scrutiny of Africa the more diffuse it becomes,
because Africa extends its roots and branches far
beyond the seas that surround it.

Africa is everywhere. It is in our genes, our
dreams, our memories, our barely expressible
aspirations, the blood terrors from which we

run. Africa is everywhere, and it may be many things, but it is not a single thing. Africa houses many families; many are black, many are non-black; some are Christian, some Muslim, some Jewish, and some, for lack of a better term, animist. Many of these families hold great enmity for one another, while others share great love. Africa is a place of golden myths as well as a place as common as the grasses which thrive upon its veldts. One cannot thumb through a book such as this and walk away from it with the notion that one has received some unified notion of the "African mind." No one people, no one continent, no one history can ever be contained within the confines of any one volume, nor any set of volumes, particularly with respect to Africa. The very word is rife with controversies. Who belongs to Africa? To whom does Africa belong? Just who is genuinely African?

And so, before I began this book, I had to ask myself whether it was right or just or sensible to include a number of quotes by Africans of European, Arabic, or Asian descent. To do so would surely offend a certain number of Afro-centrists who would argue that such a thing invalidates this book, makes a mockery of a proud and noble heritage. But those who attempt to lump Africa's some fifty-two countries and fifteen hundred cultures (not to mention the satellite cultures that span the globe) into something that can be spoken of as sourced in a single heritage are giving the African multiverse short shrift. Besides, to purposely eschew "non-black" Africa, others would argue, smacks of the racism against which black people have been fighting for millennia.

In the end, what I decided to do was close my eyes to the various "colors" of the great minds contained herein, and attend to only the content of what those great minds have to say. Let me give you an example. In Madagascar it is said, "The love of money is the tail of witch-craft," while among the Nupe it is said, "Money kills more people than a club." There is a Berber saying that runs, "Everything will satisfy you except money, as much as you have, so much more you'll want." And the Sothos (Se-Soto) say, "Wealth is a fog which soon is dispersed." It is not that there is something distinctly African about any of these proverbs. They're no more African or non-African than the European proverb, "Money is the root of all evil." Rather, wisdom is wisdom, and these are wisdoms that came into being on the continent of Africa. Wisdoms that were carried on the four winds to

Europe, the Americas, the West Indies, and beyond.

Perhaps, though, if I go on, I'll end up in more hot water than I might already be. I'll end up like the Nigerian hunter who goes into the bush and finds an old human skull. The hunter says, almost to himself, "Well, my friend, what brought you here?" But the skull answers, "Talking brought me here." The alarmed hunter runs off. He runs to the king, and tells the king, "I found a human skull in the bush. Dry as dust, it is, but it speaks like you or me!"

The king says, "Never has man born of woman ever seen such a thing." And he summons the Alkali, the Saba, and the Degi and asks them if they or the ancestors have ever heard of such a thing. None of these wise ones had ever heard of such a thing and they suggest that the king send the hunter, along with his best four guards, into the bush to retrieve this miraculous bone. The king says to the hunter, "If it be true what you say, young hunter, I will make you wealthy, but if it be false, you will be killed where you stand."

The guards accompany the hunter into the bush, and soon they come upon the very skull. The hunter says, "Brother skull, I greet you." But the skull doesn't speak. "I say, brother skull.

What brought you here?" Still the skull does not speak. Beads of sweat fly from the hunter's forehead. "Brother skull," he says, "will you not speak?" But the skull does not speak. The guards, being merciful, wait till evening. The five men eat and rest. They tell stories of other miraculous things they have seen and heard, but by and by they demand that the hunter induce the skull to speak, but the skull remains still as death. The guards draw lots and one of them kills the hunter. When the guards are gone and the night becomes full, the skull rolls toward the dead hunter's head, and says, "Brother flesh and skull, what brings you here?" The dead hunter's head replies, "Talking brought me here."

Reginald McKnight
Baltimore, Maryland

Key to the African Tribes

Africa is linguistically and culturally the most diverse continent on the planet. There are over fifteen hundred tribes, all of which vary tremendously as one spans the continent. Although we could not represent every culture in this book, the following is a list of the tribes that are represented throughout these pages.

TRIBE	ORIGIN
Amharic	Ethiopia
Ashanti	Ivory Coast
Bakongo	Zaire
Bambara	Senigal
Bantu	Southern Africa
Basa	Liberia & Nigeria
Basoto	Lesotho
Batswana	Botswana
Bemba	Northern Zimbabwe
Bondei	Kenya

TRIBE	ORIGIN
Chagga	Tanzania
Duala	Cameroon
Efik	Nigeria
Ewe	Ghana
Fanti	Ghana
Ga	Ghana
Galla	Ethiopia
Ganda	Uganda
Hausa	Northern Nigeria
Ho (Ewe)	Togo
Hutu	Wranda
Ibo	Nigeria
Ila	Northern Zimbabwe
Jabo	Liberia
Jukun	Nigeria
Kamba	Kenya
Kanuri (Bornu)	Nothern Nigeria
Kikuyu (Gikuyu)	Kenya
Kru	Liberia
Kweli	Cameroon
Lango	Uganda
Ndebele	South Africa
Ndanga	Namibia
Ndau	Mozambique
Ngone	Malawi
Nupe	Northern Nigeria

Tribe	Origin
Nyang	Cameroon
Nyoro	Uganda
Nzima	Ivory Coast
Oji (Ashanti)	Ivory Coast
Pedi	South Africa
Shona	South Africa
Songe (Kongo)	Mozambique
Sotho	LeSotho
Sumer	Sumeria (antiquity)
Suriname	South America
Swahili	Kenya
Tamashek	Central Sahara
Tiv (Munshi)	Benin and Nigeria
Toucouleure	Senegal, Mauritania
Tsonga	Mozambique
Tumbulca	Malawi
Vai	Liberia and Sierra Leone
Wolof	Senegal
Xhosa	South Africa
Yoruba	Southern Nigeria
Zulu	South Africa

1

The Breast of the Earth

AFRICA AND AFRICANITY

The strongest gods are African. I tell you it's certain they could fly and they did what they liked with their witchcraft. I don't know how they permitted slavery. The truth is, I start thinking, and I can't make head or tail of it. To my mind it all started with the scarlet handkerchiefs, the day they crossed the wall. There was an old wall in Africa, right around the coast, made of palm bark and magic insects which stung like the devil. For years they frightened away all the whites who tried to set foot in Africa. It was the scarlet that did in the Africans; the kings saw that the whites . . . were taking out these scarlet handkerchiefs as if they were waving, they told the blacks, "Go on then, go and get a scarlet handkerchief," and the blacks were so excited by the scarlet they ran down to the ships like sheep and they were captured. The Negro has always liked scarlet.

ESTEBAN MONTEJO

Even the most incorrigible maverick has to be born somewhere. He may leave the group that produced him — he may be forced to — but nothing will efface his origins, the marks of which he carries with him everywhere.

JAMES BALDWIN

Black, Negro, African American, colored, etc., etc. — we sometimes answer to but never internalize completely because they are inadequate to describe the sense of common ground we exchange at this moment. We acknowledge the miracle and disgrace of our history in the twinkling of an eye, many, many times a day as we meet each other, nodding or speaking or touching or just passing by, seemingly without a glance. Our ancient styles of gliding through the air can say enough, say everything that needs to be said. We are linked. I know something about you and you know something about me. Personal, intimate, revealing knowledge though we may never have set eyes on one another before nor will again.

JOHN EDGAR WIDEMAN

The man who emerged from the African chrysalis was a courageous, warlike individual. He was not soft; he was hard. He had fought the tsetse fly, the mosquitoes and hundreds of nameless insects and he survived. He had wrested from the hungry jungle gaps of land and had found time to think beautiful thoughts and to make beautiful things.

LERONE BENNET

The various cultures of people of color often seem very attractive to white people. (Yes, we are wonderful, we can't deny it.) But white people should not make a playground out of other people's cultures. We are not quaint. We are not exotic. We are not cool.

AMOJA THREE RIVERS

Rather a negro heart without words than negro words without heart.

BAKONGO

American culture ... is, I think, essentially black. From rock and roll, to language, to the things that young white kids aspire to be. When they think of cool, their definition of cool comes from what is cool for black people. . . .

EDDY L. HARRIS

Black will blacken people.

NYANG

Everybody can blush. Everybody can bruise. Everybody can tan and get sunburned. Everybody.

AMOJA THREE RIVERS

The black man has a rib and a cup of blood more than the white man.

MOROCCO

If there had been no poverty in Europe, then the white man would not have come to spread his clothes in Africa.

OJI

We live surrounded by white images, and white in this world is synonymous with the good, light, beauty, success, so that, despite ourselves sometimes, we run after that whiteness and deny our darkness, which has been made into the symbol of all that is evil and inferior.

PAULE MARSHALL

People of the same blood eat from the same pot.

SOTHO

Anything I have ever learned of any conse-
quence, I have learned from black people. I have
never been bored by any black person, ever.

TONI MORRISON

What our girls and women have a right to
demand from our best men is that they cease to
imitate the artificial standards of other people
and create a race standard for their own.

FANNIE BARRIER WILLIAMS

It is within the race where integration is not
only needed, but mandatory. We shall remain a
weak people until we begin the drive for integration of blacks first of all, instead of battling to
integrate with other peoples.

CHANCELLOR WILLIAMS

The world is white no longer, and it will never
be white again.

JAMES BALDWIN

But I am not tragically colored. There is no great
sorrow dammed up in my soul, not lurking
behind my eyes. I do not mind at all. I do not
belong to the sobbing school of negrohood who
hold that nature somehow has given them a

lowdown dirty deal and whose feelings are all hurt about it. Even in the helter-skelter skirmish that is my life, I have seen that the world is to the strong regardless of a little pigmentation more or less. No, I do not weep at the world — I am too busy sharpening my oyster knife.

ZORA NEALE HURSTON

The African race is an India rubber ball; the harder you dash it to the ground, the higher it will rise.

BANTU

Europeans created and popularized the image of Africa as a jungle, a wild place where people were cannibals, naked and savage in a country-side overrun with dangerous animals. Such an image of the Africans was so hateful to Afro-Americans that they refused to identify with Africa. We did not realize that in hating Africa and the Africans we were hating ourselves. You cannot hate the roots of a tree and not hate the tree itself.

MALCOLM X

One finger can't catch a mother louse.

NYANG

Foreigners may call us a nation of busybodies,

but to us an individual's life belongs to the community and not just to him or her. So a person has no right to take his or her life while another member of the community looks on. He must interfere. He must stop it from happening.

BUCHI EMECHETA

When black man steal him steal half a bit; but when white man steal him steal a whole sugar plantation.

JAMAICA

You think dark is just one color, but it ain't. They're five or six kinds of blacks. Some silky, some wooly. Some just empty. Some like fingers. And it don't stay still. It moves and changes from one kind of black to another. Saying something is pitch black is like saying something is green. What kind of green? Green like my bottles? Green like a grasshopper? Green like a cucumber, lettuce, or green like the sky is just before it breaks loose to storm? Well, night black is the same way. Might as well be a rainbow.

TONI MORRISON

Equal rights and equal justice will never come from appeals to the mighty, and granted as an Act of Grace, but only from their own position of power and influence which develop from a united people engaged in great and vast undertakings of their own. If we fail to accept this challenge at this critical turning point in our history, we will have proved ourselves unworthy of having any descendants, and our very names should be forgotten by them — or cursed by the farthest generation.

CHANCELLOR WILLIAMS

I am because we are, and since we are therefore I am.

JOHN MBITI

Africa is never the same to anyone who leaves it and returns again. It is not a land of changes, but it is a land of moods, and its moods are numberless. It is not fickle, but because it has mothered not only men, but races, and cradles not only cities, but civilizations — and seen them die, and see new ones born again — Africa can be dispassionate, indifferent, warm, or cynical, replete with the weariness of too much wisdom.

BERYL MARKHAM

Zion me wan go home,
Zion me wan go home,
Oh, oh,
Zion me wan go home,

Africa, me wan fe go,
Africa, me wan fe go,
Oh, oh,
Africa, me wan fe go,

Take me back to Et'iopea lan,
Take me back to Et'iopea lan,
Oh, oh,
Take me back to Et'iopea lan,

Zion me wan go home,
Zion me wan go home,
Oh, oh,
Zion me wan go home.

RASTAFARIAN CHANT

From the Bottom
to the Top

YOUTH AND AGE

The young are overhanging rocks; the old are
trees on the edge of a precipice; no one knows
which will fall first.

MADAGASCAR

Honor a child and it will honor you.

ILA

Grown people know that they do not always
know the why of things, and even if they think
they know, they do not know where and how
they got the proof. Hence the irritation they
show when the children keep on demanding to
know if a thing is so and how the grown folks

got the proof of it. It is so troublesome ... to the pigeonhole way of life.

ZORA NEALE HURSTON

That's what being young is all about. You have the courage and the daring to think that you can make a difference. You're not prone to measure your energies in time. You're not likely to live by equations.

RUBY DEE

Make a bed for the children of other people in the place where your own children sleep.

MOROCCO

Where there is an old man nothing need go wrong.

SWAHILI

Children are the wisdom of the nation.

JABO

Age gives a man some things with the right hand even as it takes away others with the left. The torrent of the old man's water may no longer smash into the hole of the roadside tree a full stride away as it once did ... but in return the eye of his mind is given wing to fly way beyond the familiar sights of his homestead.

CHINUA ACHEBE

When mother cow is chewing grass its young ones watch its mouth.

IBO

Where there is a head, one doesn't put the head-dress on the knee. [Where there is an old man, one doesn't ask the advice of a young man.]

HO

Before one has white hairs, one must first have them black.

SENEGAL

A child that asks questions isn't stupid.

EWE

A cynical young person is almost the saddest sight to see, because it means that he or she has gone from knowing nothing to believing in nothing.

MAYA ANGELOU

Even we old people must learn, and recognize that the things people know today were not born with us. No, knowledge is not a hereditary thing.

SEMBENE OUSMANE

The old men tended to see . . . apparitions more than the young ones, who hardly ever did. A young man does not have the gift of seeing much, and he rarely hears voices either.

ESTEBAN MONTEJO

There is no wealth where there are no children.

JABO

The eggs teach the hen how to hatch.

KWELI

The eggs give the hen instruction in brooding.

BANTU

It takes a whole village to raise a single child.

YORUBA

A child is like a camel's neck, it goes where it pleases.

MOROCCO

If you refuse to be made straight when you are green, you will not be made straight when you are dry.

KAMBA

If you see an old man running, either he is chasing something or something is chasing him.

NUPE

One rolls up a skin while it is still damp.

TSONGA

If with the right hand you flog the child, with your left hand draw her unto your breast.

YORUBA

An old woman is always uneasy when dry bones are mentioned in a proverb.

CHINUA ACHEBE

There is no medicinal against old age.

YORUBA

How old he is. All his old friends are dead. He's an ancestor already. A gust of wind would sweep him off his feet. Yet he lives on. I hope the spirits listen to him.

ALFRED HUTCHINSON

Old as she was, she still missed her daddy sometimes.

GLORIA NAYLOR

Everywhere, everywhere, children are the scorned of the earth.

TONI MORRISON

Father work, picknie spend.

JAMAICA

The child hates him who gives it all it wants.

WOLOF

Children suck them mother when them young, them father when them old.

JAMAICA

There was a kid went into a candy store, said, "Mister, how much are those candy bars?" The fellow said, "They are two for a quarter." Kid says, "Well, how much for one?" Fellow said, "Fifteen cent." Kid said, "Well, give me the other one."

REDD FOXX

When one grows old, one needs children to look after one. If you have no children, and your parents have gone, who can you call your own?

BUCHI EMECHETA

You need not tell a child that there is a God.

NZIMA

3

The Nearness of You

LOVE, FAMILY, FRIENDSHIP

. . . Love, god's infinite, meditate on it
    Meditate on god's
infinite love Draw close, encircle, cross
    arms, join hands,
hold silence and meditate see love shine
    shine shine Walk
right up to it, rub it on your hand.

And not just a precious and heaven
    sent But a blemished
Fallen-love love Imprecise and foul
    sloppy, impious,
blasphemous love Love tainted and
    corrupt, even Fallen

love Love, we say, can conquer.

See Love shine Like a rock Unlike a
    swift and surgical
hate No matter how exact And even
    cleansing Hate has
nothing on wonder has nothing on
    wondrous working
love. . .

JONATHON SMITH
FROM MARVIN LOVES
(IF THIS WORLD WERE MINE. . .)

Not where I was born, but where it goes well
with me is my home.

KANURI

Love paralyzes the joints.

BATSWANA

Love is the understanding that all people are
bound together in guilt and only individuals are
capable of achieving personal salvation. The
duty of every sensitive individual is to see to it
that conditions are created in which he and others like him can become the majority.

LEWIS NKOSI

A powerful friend becomes a powerful enemy.

AMHARIC

No friendship, except after enmity.

EGYPT

That which is loved by the heart is the remedy.

KENYA

We can do without our friends, but not our neighbors.

EGYPT

It seems to me that trying to live without friends is like milking a bear to get cream for your morning coffee. It is a whole lot of trouble, and then not worth much after you get it.

ZORA NEALE HURSTON

The way to the loved one is not theory.

NYANG

Whatever happens, whether you get rich or stay poor, ruin your health or live to old age, you always end up back where you started: hungry for the one thing everybody loses — young loving.

TONI MORRISON

Even a little thing brings friendship to remembrance.

GANDA

Loving one who doesn't love you is loving the rain that falls in the forest.

RUANDA

How is one to love a person by being told to love her?

SWAHILI

The disease of love has no physician.

SWAHILI

One does not love another if one does not accept anything from her.

KANURI

Don't love me as you do a door, pushed to and fro.

MADAGASCAR

He who loves you wearies you; he who hates you kills you.

MOROCCO

Whoever loves thee, even a dog, thou wilt also love.

TSONGA

To give to thy friend is not to cast away, it is to store for the future.

SWAHILI

Better to lose a little money than a little friendship.

MADAGASCAR

It is preferable to change the world on the basis

of love of mankind. But if that quality be too rare, then common sense seems to be the next best thing.

BESSIE HEAD

The heart is a marketplace.

GANDA

Make friends when you no need them.

JAMAICA

Friendship slays many evils.

GANDA

They are not all friends who grin showing their teeth.

UNITED STATES

Mutual love is often better than natural brotherhood.

BAKONGO

Better a clever enemy than a blundering friend.

SWAHILI

Friendship that is kept up only while eyes see eyes, does not go to the heart.

YORUBA

Quick loving a woman means quick not loving a woman.

YORUBA

Handsome face woman not be best kind of woman.

JAMAICA

True friendship outlives relationship.

BANTU

Let your love be like misty rain; little in coming but flooding the river.

MADAGASCAR

A wife is like a giant.

GA

Relatives are like a part of your body; if anything touches it, however small, you feel it.

HAUSA

He who pulls a branch brings the leaves with it.

ILA

God could not be everywhere so he sent Mother.

EGYPT

The source of human love is the mother.

BAKONGO

No one will sympathize with one as much as one's own mother; for, who is it will show kindness to another person's child?

YORUBA

A person can run for years but sooner or later he has to take a stand in the place which, for better or worse, he calls home, do what he can to change things there.

PAULE MARSHALL

Every river run to its mamma.

JAMAICA

The mother is she who catches the knife by the blade.

BATSWANA

It is etiquette for a son or daughter to talk to the father in a gentle and polite tone, and the parent, except when reprimanding or correcting his children, is required by custom to reciprocate the compliment in the same way as his children extend it to him.

JOMO KENYATTA
ON GIKUYU CUSTOM

There's a time when you have to explain to your children why they're born, and it's a marvelous thing if you know the reason by then.

HAZEL SCOTT

Blacks concede that hurrawing, jibing, jiving, signifying, disrespecting, cursing, even outright insults might be acceptable under particular conditions, but aspersions cast against one's family call for immediate attack.

MAYA ANGELOU

The worst thing that a man can do to infuriate another is . . . to mention his mother's name in an indecent way. This would result in a fight to defend the sacred name of the mother. The great attachment and respect shown to the mother by her children is due to the fact that she is their nurse, and has daily closer contact with them than the father. She feeds and looks after the clothing and ornaments of the children. When they are in trouble, they first go to their mother. . . .

JOMO KENYATTA

I cannot forget my mother. Though not as sturdy as others, she is my bridge. When I needed to get across, she steadied herself long enough for me to run across safely.

RENITA WEEMS

You got to hold on to your brother . . . and don't let him fall, no matter what it looks like is happening to him and no matter how evil you gets with him. You going to be evil with him many a time. . . . You may not be able to stop nothing from happening. But you got to let him know you's there.

JAMES BALDWIN

The race could not succeed, nor build strong citizens, until we have a race of women competent to do more than bear a breed of negative men.

T. THOMAS FORTUNE

What happens to your wife happens to yourself.

MADAGASCAR

Tremendous amounts of talent are being lost to our society just because that talent wears a skirt.

SHIRLEY CHISOLM

You have tampered with woman, you have struck a rock.

SOUTH AFRICAN WOMEN'S PROTEST SLOGAN

Marriage without good faith is like a teapot without a tray.

MOROCCO

Any woman who has a great deal to offer the world is in trouble. And if she's a black woman, she's in deep trouble.

HAZEL SCOTT

Woman is king.

SUDANESE

If you mistreat the woman, you reject the image of God that is the essence of her being. Thus a nation can rise no higher than its woman. ... Most people in today's world are uneasy when you begin talking about women and their gifts and powers. ... Man is in need of greater understanding of the woman, the first teacher and the first nurse of all the human family on the planet earth.

TYNNETTA MUHAMMED

The time has come, and is really long past, that our women should not have to go in the front line for freedom and justice for us. It is time now that we men stand up and be counted for the liberation of our people in America ... the world.

MINISTER LOUIS FARRAKHAN

The way to the beloved is not thorny.

DUALA

Against the goodness of woman the sadness of man is also good.

ETHIOPIA

A house may hold a hundred men, but the heart of a woman has only room for one of them.

EGYPT

Tell me whom you love, I'll tell you who you are.

CREOLE

Men — all they were interested in were male babies to keep their names going. But did not a woman have to bear the woman-child who would later bear the sons? "God, when will you create a woman who will be fulfilled in herself, a full human being, not anybody's appendage?"

BUCHI EMECHETA

It takes a long time to be really married. One marries many times at many levels within a marriage. If you have more marriages than you have divorces within the marriage, you're lucky and you stick it out.

RUBY DEE

If you wish to be blamed, marry; if you wish to be praised, die.

GALLA

Marriage has teeth and him bite very hot.

JAMAICA

Before you marry, keep both eyes open; after you marry, shut one.

JAMAICA

A land abused becomes a burial place; a spouse

not desired you become old with.

MADAGASCAR

The long-term accommodation that protects marriage and other such relationships is . . . for-getfulness.

ALICE WALKER

Buttocks rubbing together do not lack sweat.

ILA

The question is not now with the woman, "How shall I cramp, stunt and simplify and nullify myself to make me eligible to the honor of being swallowed up into some little man?" but the problem . . . rests with the man as to how he can develop . . . to reach the ideal of a generation of women who demand the noblest, the grand-est and best achievements of which he is capable.

ANNA JULIA COOPER

Seven children won't hold a husband, but plenty of wisdom will.

MADAGASCAR

He who has children is he who has blessings.

TOUCOULEURE

He who leaves a child lives eternally.

CHAGGA

Youth gangs in the street, on the corner, that murder their own youth, that don't play, don't waste energy seeking fathers, don't need anyone telling them who they are or what to do because they manufacture and enforce their own rules, step into the vacuum and become their own rules, step into the vacuum and become their own fathers and mothers, creating a world where childhood has disappeared, where the idea of fathers and sons is anachronistic, redundant. For these sons there is no past or future, only the sheer exhilaration and terror of now, the only time that counts, the only time you're ever alive.

JOHN EDGAR WIDEMAN

The town is a barren wilderness to one who is unhappy in one's homelife.

YORUBA

The ties established between two families by a happy marriage are stronger than those of money.

TSONGA

To be too much married makes you say, "There's immorality about." [People in glass houses should not throw stones.]

BONDEI

You need double strength if you quarrel with a woman whose husband is absent.

SHONA

A child who has a mother eats a second time.

BONDEI

Out of the corner of my eye I could see my mother. Out of the corner of the other eye, I could see her shadow on the wall, cast there by the lamplight. It was a big and solid shadow, and it looked so much like my mother that I became frightened. For I could not be sure whether for the rest of my life I would be able to tell when it was really my mother and when it was really her shadow standing between me and the rest of the world.

JAMAICA KINCAID

The greatness of love obliterates conventions.

SOTHO

Faith dares everything, and love hears everything.

JAMAICA

To marry is to put a snake in one's handbag.

TSONGA

Love, I find is like singing. Everybody can do

enough to satisfy themselves, though it may not impress the neighbors as being very much.

ZORA NEALE HURSTON

We love because it's the only true adventure.

NIKKI GIOVANNI

It's some who tries to spread love . . .
    and, I think love will always win.
    Always.
But . . . what fight it must make.

J. CALIFORNIA COOPER

By loving your enemy, I don't mean letting people commit crimes against others without stopping them. I mean one should never hate them or despise them. Real love brings us all to the same level.

LEWIS NKOSI

Love has no disputing.

KIKUYU

Love is two people . . . feeding each other, not one living on the soul of the other, like a ghost.

BESSIE HEAD

You may condemn the one you love, but you pay his fine for him.

UNITED STATES

A jealous love can be a little amusing. In fact, jealousy made evident in a room filled with people can be an outright intoxicant to everyone, including the lovers. It must be remembered, however, that jealousy in romance is like salt in food. A little can enhance the savor, but too much can spoil the pleasure and, under certain circumstances, can be life-threatening.

MAYA ANGELOU

The heart cannot hold two.

EGYPT

There is always something left to love. And if you ain't learned that, you ain't learned nothing.

LORRAINE HANSBERRY

There is a loneliness that can be rocked. Arms crossed, knees drawn up; holding on, this motion, unlike a ship's, smooths and contains the rockers. It's an inside kind — wrapped tight like skin.

TONI MORRISON

A long spell of rheumatism is apt to point out your best friends.

UNITED STATES

The man who is not jealous in love, loves not.

TAMASHEK

Jealousy was boiled in the same pot as a stone; the stone got soft and jealousy remained.

DUALA

Love and cough never hide.

JAMAICA

Mother is gold.

YORUBA

Sticks in a bundle are unbreakable.

BONDEI

God created us so that we should form the human family, existing together because we were made for one another. We are not made for an exclusive self-sufficiency but for interdependence, and we break the law of being at our peril.

DESMOND TUTU

4

Uhuru's Fire

CREATIVITY, BEAUTY, ART

God made the sea, we make the ship; He made the wind, we make the sail; He made the calm, we make oars.

SWAHILI

Verily, beauty is power.

KANURI

If you suffer in order to be beautiful, don't blame anyone but yourself.

GANDA

The bird caught in the trap is the one to sing sweetly.

OJI

Everybody is influenced by somebody or something. If there is an original who is the original?

ERNESTINE ANDERSON

One should be able to return to the first sentence of a novel and find the resonances of the entire work.

GLORIA NAYLOR

Every society is really governed by hidden laws, by unspoken but profound assumptions on the part of the people, and ours is no exception. It is up to the American writer to find out what these laws and assumptions are.

JAMES BALDWIN

Blues is a basis of historical continuity for black people. It is a ritualized way of talking about ourselves and passing it on.

SHERLEY ANNE WILLIAMS

People wish to be poets more than they wish to write poetry and that's a mistake. One should wish to celebrate more than one wishes to be celebrated.

LUCILLE CLIFTON

The average man doesn't want to have to use his brain when he listens to music. Music should wash away the dust of his everyday life.

ART BLAKEY

A writer needs certain conditions in which to work and create art. She needs a piece of time; a peace of mind; a quiet place; and a private life.

MARGARET WALKER

The beauty you left behind you, where will you find it tomorrow?

MOROCCO

The artistic innovator is perhaps our society's most valuable citizen. He or she does not so much change the world, as change how we view it. They are ambassadors of peace and advocates of understanding. They melt our differences into the common ground of the dance floor, the theater, the concert hall, and a million living rooms across the nation. That is why it is important that we so diligently search for them.

OSSIE DAVIS

I have a great belief in the fact that whenever there is chaos, it creates wonderful thinking. I consider chaos a gift.

SEPTIMA POINSETTE CLARK

Art is the only thing you cannot punch a button for. You must do it the old-fashioned way. Stay up and really burn the midnight oil. There are no compromises.

LEONTYNE PRICE

Slowly, slowly one must stalk the monkey through the bush.

WOLOF

Softly, softly ketch monkey.

JAMAICA

Slowly, slowly will catch the monkey.

JABO

Art is not for the cultivated taste. It is to cultivate taste.

NIKKI GIOVANNI

We should not have a tin cup out for something as important as the arts in this country, the richest in the world. Creative artists are always begging, but always being used when it's time to show us at our best.

LEONTYNE PRICE

All I know about music is that not many people ever really hear it. And even then, on the rare occasions when something opens within, and the music enters, what we mainly hear, or hear corroborated, are personal, private, vanishing evocations. But the man who creates the music is hearing something else, is dealing with the roar rising from the void and imposing order on it as it hits the air. What is evoked in him, then is of another order, more terrible because it has no words, and triumphant, too, for that same reason. And his triumph, when he triumphs, is ours ... how awful the relationship must be between the musician and his instrument. He has to fill it, this instrument, with the breath of life, his own. He has to make it do what he wants it to do. And a piano is just a piano. It's made out of so much wood and wires and little hammers and big ones, and ivory. While there's only so much you can do with it, the only way to find this out is to try — to try and make it do everything.

JAMES BALDWIN

There is no beauty but in relationships. Nothing cut off by itself is beautiful. Never can things in destructive relationships be beautiful. All beauty is in the creative purpose of our relationships; all ugliness is in the destructive aims of the destroyer's arrangements.

AYI KWEI ARMAH

In crooked wood one recognizes the artist.

EWE

Beauty is in the oleander and the oleander is bitter.

MOROCCO

All along the lake the larks
send their sweet scat through the air.
It's April. New weather jazzes the leaves
The late sun — a long note blown
across the water. Near shore
a tadpole itching for legs.

TIM SEIBLES

5

Sticks and Stones

CONFLICT, TROUBLE, VIOLENCE

Back of the problem of race and color lies a greater problem which both obscures and implements it; and that is the fact that so many civilized persons are willing to live in comfort even if the price of this is poverty, ignorance and disease of the majority of their fellowmen; that to maintain this privilege men have waged war until today war tends to become universal and continuous, and the excuse for this war continues largely to be color and race.

W.E.B. DuBois

Race, what is that? Race is a competition, somebody winning and somebody losing. . . . Blood doesn't run in races! Come on!

BEAH RICHARDS

Laughter gives confidence; its absence causes dispute.

TAMASHEK

Racism is so universal in this country, so widespread and deep-seated that it is invisible because it is normal.

SHIRLEY CHISOLM

Fright is worse than a blow.

MOROCCO

Fear has laughter in it; fierceness has mournings.

NYANG

What difference do it make if the thing you scared of is real or not?

TONI MORRISON

We remain in that position . . . anticipating happiness in that unhappy architectural shame — the ghetto. Our eyes dart apprehensively, on the lookout for those of our brothers who have resorted to the insanity of crime to protest their insane conditions. For, indeed, if we were not scared of moral ridicule we would regard crime as a form of protest. Is not man with a hungry stomach in the same position as man whose land has been taken away from him? What if he is a victim of both?

MANGO TSHABANGU

To take revenge is often to sacrifice oneself.

BAKONGO

Hungry people cannot be good at learning or producing anything, except perhaps violence.

PEARL BAILEY

Nonviolent passive resistance is effective as long as your opposition adheres to the same rules as you do. But if peaceful protest is met with violence, its efficacy is at an end. For me, non-violence was not a moral principle but a strategy; there is no moral goodness in using an ineffective weapon.

NELSON MANDELA

Blows returned never hurt.

CREOLE

You no hear with your ears you hear with your skin.

JAMAICA

The sweat of a brave man is blood.

PEDI

We will either find a way or make one.

HANNIBAL

Now when you hates you shrinks up inside and gets littler and you squeezes your heart tight and you stays so mad. With peoples you feels sick all the time like you needs the doctor.

MARGARET WALKER

Hate has no medicine.

GA

When the white man is about to leave the garden for good, he wrecks it.

YORUBA

Nobody says it's pretty here; nobody says it's easy either. What it is is decisive, and if you pay attention to the street plans, all laid out, the City can't hurt you.

TONI MORRISON

The knife does not know its owner.

NDAU

You may drink from a human skull, but you can never obliterate from your mind that it once had eyes in it.

BAKONGO

Sometimes prejudice is like a hair across your cheek. You can't see it, you can't find it with your fingers, but you keep brushing at it because the feel of it is irritating.

MARIAN ANDERSON

Such a wave of hate is being planted up deeper in this world. The devil is the busiest thing I know.

J. CALIFORNIA COOPER

Racism is easy to see, hard to prove, impossible to deny.

ANONYMOUS

He who throws stones in the night kills his brother.

EWE

If you want to get at the root of murder . . . you have to look for the blacksmith who made the hatchet.

EWE

How does the poor man retain his calm in the face of such provocation? From what bottomless wells of patience does he draw? His great good humor must explain it. This sense of humor turned sometimes against himself, must be what saves him from total dejection. He has learned to squeeze every drop of enjoyment he can out of his stony luck. And the fool who oppresses him will make a particular point of that enjoyment: You see, they are not the least like ourselves. They don't read and can't use the luxuries that you and I must have. They have the animal capacity to endure the pain of, shall we say, domestication. The very words the white master had said in his time about the black race as a whole. Now we say them about the poor.

CHINUA ACHEBE

Endurance pierces marble.

MOROCCO

The man who goes ahead stumbles that the man who follows may have his wits about him.

BONDEI

Our misfortunes are never out of proportion to our capacity to bear them.

YORUBA

Okonkwo ruled his household with a heavy hand. His wives, especially the youngest, lived in perpetual fear of his own fiery temper, and so did his little children. Perhaps down in his heart Okonkwo was not a cruel man. But his whole life was dominated by fear, the fear of failure and weakness. It was deeper and more intimate than the fear of the forest, and of the forces of nature . . .

CHINUA ACHEBE

I'll have to, as you say, take a stand — something toward shaking up that system. . . . Despair . . . is too easy an out.

PAULE MARSHALL

The attacks of the wild beast cannot be averted with only bare hands.

SOUTH AFRICA

When two elephants struggle it is the grass that suffers.

SWAHILI

In the house of the coward there is no weeping.

PEDI

Mediocrity is safe.

NIKKI GIOVANNI

For people sometimes believed that it was safer to live with complaints, was necessary to cooperate with grief, was all right to become an accomplice in self-ambush . . . took heart to flat-out decide to be well and stride into the future sane and whole.

TONI CADE BAMBARA

Coward man keeps sound bone.

CREOLE

An elephant doesn't die of one broken rib.

TSONGA

Endure, and drink your medicine.

KENYA

Man you can't beat you have to call him your friend.

JAMAICA

The lion which kills is not the one that roars.

XHOSA

Wear out, body! Remain, o heart.

NDEBELE

6

Let the Trumpet Sound

DEATH, TRANSITION, ETERNITY

Death ain't nothing. . . . Death ain't nothing but a fastball on the outside corner. . . . You get one of them fastballs, about waist high, over the outside corner of the plate where you can get the meat of that bat on it . . . and good god! You can kiss it good-bye.

AUGUST WILSON

The world is big but the dead are bigger. We've been dying since the beginning; the living try but the gap always widens.

WOLE SOYINKA

Fear is no obstacle to death.

BAMBARA

Strength does not prevent a man from dying.

KIKUYU

The last time you're doing something — knowing you're doing it for the last — makes it even more alive than the first.

GLORIA NAYLOR

But I'm gettin ready to go. How am I doin it? I'm layin aside every weight and sin that does so easily beset me and I'm gettin light for the flight.

WILLIE MAE FORD SMITH

If the Nile knows your secret it will soon be in the desert.

AMHARIC

It is the heart which carries one to Hell or to Heaven.

KANURI

Death has the key to open the miser's chest.

OJI

A man dies before we appreciate him.

JABO

We were afraid of the dead because we never would tell when they might show up again.

JAMAICA KINCAID

The criminal arms which beat him down were deceived. It was not in the tomb that he lay, but in the hearts of all men and women. He was present in the evening when the fires were lit in the rice fields. ... He preceded the sowing of the crops, he was present during the rainy season and he kept company with the young people at harvest time.

SEMBENE OUSMAN

A person is always thanked after death.

BATSWANA

Just then, Death finished his prowling through the house on his padded feet and entered the room. He bowed to Mama in his way, and she made her manners and left us to act out our ceremonies over unimportant things.

ZORA NEALE HURSTON

Never depend too much on the blackberry blossoms.

UNITED STATES

Dying is cleaning, like the broom.

MADAGASCAR

The morning of one's life foreshadows the eve.

YORUBA

Against the illness of death there is no medicine.

TOUCOULEUR

The priest will die; the doctor will depart this life; the sorcerer will not be spared.

YORUBA

Death has no heifer.

ILA

His eyes are as big as a food bowl, round like moons and red like fire; and they are rolling about like ripe fruit clanging in his mind. The teeth in his mouth look like lion's fangs, and they are bright red, for it is not yam he likes, nor bananas, nor okra, nor bitter leaf; he likes nothing but human flesh.

D. O. FAGUNWA

Always being in a hurry doesn't hinder death, neither does going slowly hinder living.

SWAHILI

Death is hiding in the corner of the blanket. [Death is everywhere.]

BASOTO

Eternal death has worked like a warrior rat, with diabolical sense of duty, to gnaw my bottom. Everything is finished now.

AMA ATA AIDOO

Death is the pursuer, disease the constant companion of people.

MADAGASCAR

Death is blind.

TSONGA

All this is to do with the spirit world, and we should face it without fear. The living are more dangerous. . . . That's the way to look at it, fairly and squarely. If a dead person comes up to you, don't run away, ask him, "What do you want, brother?" He will either answer you or take you away with him somewhere. . . .

ESTEBAN MONTEJO

Death gives no answer.

JABO

Whatever you do you will die.

VAI

7

Jumping at the Sun, Walking on the Sea

CHARACTER, VIRTUES, VALUES

Mama exhorted her children at every opportunity to "jump at de sun." We might not land on the sun, but at least we would get off the ground.

ZORA NEALE HURSTON

No one can leave his character behind him when he goes on a journey.

YORUBA

Because it rained the day the egg was hatched the foolish chicken swore he was a fish.

WOLE SOYINKA

Don't break down bridge you just crossed.

JAMAICA

Just hold up your end of the beam an' the world'll roll on.

UNITED STATES

If your intention is pure you can walk on the sea.

SWAHILI

He who desires to attain things must pass through many nights.

TUNISIAN

The thing that makes you exceptional, if you are at all, is inevitably that which must also make you lonely.

LORRAINE HANSBERRY

The smaller the lizard the greater its chance of becoming a crocodile.

AMHARIC

Abundance in the world becomes great with good faith.

MOROCCO

He who hopes fares better than he who wishes, and he who wishes fares better than he who despairs.

MOROCCO

In the gate of patience there is no crowding.

MOROCCO

We spend most of our days preventing the heart from beating out its greatness. The things we would rather encourage lie choking among the weeds of our restrictions. And before we know it, time has eluded us. There is not much time allotted us, and half of that we sleep. While we are awake we should allow our hearts to bear the shame of being seen living.

EFUA T. SUTHERLAND

Until the last gourd has been broken, let us not talk of drought.

YORUBA

What is a cynic but a romanticist turned sour.

LEWIS NKOSI

You can't be nobody but who you are ... that shadow wasn't nothing but you growing into yourself. You either got to grow into it or cut it down to fit you. But that's all you got to make life with. That's all you got to measure yourself

81

against that world out there.

AUGUST WILSON

The heart is like deep waters.

TSONGA

He who has fine clothes should also have shabby ones.

SURINAME

Pride only goes the length one can spit.

BAKONGO

I don't criticize others so that others may not criticize me.

SONGE (KONGO)

When you have been bitten by a snake you flee from a worm.

BASA

Mistakes ain't haystacks, or they'd be more fat ponies than they is.

UNITED STATES

The man who tie mad dog is the right somebody to loose him.

JAMAICA

The journey of folly has to be traveled a second time.

BONDEI

Habit is a full-grown mountain, hard to get over or pull down.

BAKONGO

We have rarely been encouraged and equipped to appreciate the fact that the truth works, that it releases the Spirit and that it is a joyous thing.

TONI CADE BAMBARA

You never find yourself until you face the truth.

PEARL BAILEY

You catch cow by him horn, but man by him word.

JAMAICA

Every man honest till the day they catch him.

JAMAICA

Man that no tell lie, hair grow on him hand middle.

JAMAICA

Mouth not keeping to mouth and lip not keeping to lip, bring trouble to the jaws.

YORUBA

He that forgives gains the victory.

YORUBA

A man is his words.

KRU

"Mr. Mouth" hurt his master.

YAO

The voice of truth is easily known.

WOLOF

Silence produces peace and peace produces safety.

SWAHILI

Cursing follows gossip.

SHONA

If you are a liar, recollect.

EGYPT

In the midst of your illness you will promise a goat, but when you recover, a chicken will seem sufficient.

JUKUN

A promise is a debt.

SWAHILI

People do not wish to appear foolish; to avoid the appearance of foolishness, they were willing to remain actually fools.

ALICE WALKER

A fool is a treasure to the wise.

BATSWANA

There are forty kinds of lunacy, but only one kind of common sense.

BANTU

When the fool does not succeed in bleaching ebony he tries to blacken ivory.

AMHARIC

A nice man ... a nice, neighborly, everybody-knows him man. The kind you let in your house because he was not dangerous, because you had seen him with children ... and never heard a scrap of gossip about him doing wrong. Felt not only safe but kindly in his company because he was the sort women ran to when they thought they were being followed, or watched, or needed someone to have the extra key just in case you locked yourself out. He was the man who took you to your door if you missed the trolley and had to walk street at night. Who warned young girls away from hooch joints and the man who lingered there. Women teased him because they trusted him ... he knew wrong wasn't right, and did it anyway.

TONI MORRISON

A smooth lie is better than a course truth.

EGYPT

Gossiping and lying are brother and sister.

KENYA

He who cultivates in secret is betrayed by the smoke.

CHAGGA

Smoke rises from beneath every roof.

BAMBARA

The earth is a beehive; we all enter by the same door but live in different cells.

BANTU

Those who are buried in the same grave don't insult each other.

HUTU

When the calabash falls to the ground, the ladle shouldn't laugh.

HO

The eye is a thief.

EFIK

At the bottom of patience there is heaven.

KAMBA

Avarice destroys what the avaricious gathers.

BATSWANA

And she had nothing to fall back on; not

maleness, not whiteness, not ladyhood, not anything. And out of profound desolation of her
reality she may very well have invented herself.

TONI MORRISON

The man who suffers much knows much.

HO

Wisdom is not a medicine to be swallowed.

BAKONGO

Foolishness often precedes wisdom.

BAKONGO

If there was no fool, cunning man couldn't live.

JAMAICA

There is medicine for madness, but not for foolishness.

SWAHILI

I have been in Sorrow's kitchen and licked out
all the pots. Then I have stood on the peaky
mountain wrapped in rainbows, with a harp and
a sword in my hands.

ZORA NEALE HURSTON

Never be afraid to sit awhile and think.

LORRAINE HANSBERRY

Service is the rent you pay for room on this

earth.

SHIRLEY CHISHOLM

There is nothing to make you like other human beings so much as doing things for them.

ZORA NEALE HURSTON

Beautify your tongue, you will attain what you desire.

MOROCCO

Hope does not disappoint.

XHOSA

There is an incredible amount of magic and feistiness in black men that nobody has been able to wipe out. But everybody has tried.

TONI MORRISON

An envious heart makes a treacherous ear.

ZORA NEALE HURSTON

Kindness can pluck the hairs of a lion's mustache.

SUDANESE

The patient one becomes the victor.

TOUCOULEUR

Avoid fried meats which angry up the blood. If your stomach disputes you, lie down and pacify it with cool thoughts. Keep the juices jangling around gently as you move. Go lightly on the vices, such as carrying on in society. The social ramble ain't restful. Avoid running at all times. Don't look back. Something might be gaining on you.

SATCHEL PAIGE

The indolent person reckons religious fasting a labor.

YORUBA

I believe in the brotherhood of all men, but I don't believe in wasting brotherhood on anyone who doesn't want to practice it with me. Brotherhood is a two-way street. I don't think brotherhood should be practiced with a man just because his skin is white. Brotherhood should hinge upon the deeds and attitudes of a man.

MALCOLM X

To a haughty belly, kindness is hard to swallow and harder to digest.

ZORA NEALE HURSTON

When a man says to his character, "Stay here and wait for me," scarcely has he turned his back than his character is close on his heels.

AMADOU KOUMBA

I would not know how to be a human being at all, except I learned this from other human beings. We are made for a delicate network of relationships, of interdependence. Not even the most powerful nation can be completely self-sufficient.

DESMOND TUTU

You may well cry. But this is nothing
To beat your breast. It was how
We all began and will end. A child,
Once out of the womb, will shout,
Even like the chick or seedling
Out of its shell. And whether
For pain, for laugh, who can tell? But
    now you
Have lived to this day, perhaps you are
    ripe
To hazard a crack at life's nut. Still,
Do not, my people, venture overmuch
Else in unraveling the knot, you
Entangle yourselves. It is enough
You know now that each day we live
Hints at why we cried out at birth.

JOHN PEPPER CLARK

8

Tell Me What I Say

HISTORY AND OTHER STORIES

It is the story that can continue beyond the war and warrior. It is the story that outlives the sound of war-drums and the exploits of brave fighters. It is the story, not the others, that saves our progeny from blundering like blind beggars into the spikes of the cactus fence. The story is our escort; without it we are blind. Does the blind man own his escort? No, neither do we the story; rather it is the thing that owns us and directs us. It is the thing that makes us different from cattle; it is the mark on the face that sets one people apart from their neighbors.

CHINUA ACHEBE

An old story does not open the ear as a new one does.

YORUBA

When you go to the donkey house don't talk about ears.

JAMAICA

Teach your children they are the direct descendants of the greatest of the greatest and proudest race who ever peopled the earth. . . . Sojourner Truth is worthy of the place of sainthood alongside Joan of Arc; Crispus Atticus and George William Gordon are entitled to the halo of martyrdom with no less glory than that of any other race. Toussaint L'Ouverture's brilliancy as a soldier and statesman outshone that of Cromwell, Napoleon and Washington; hence he is entitled to the highest place as a hero among men.

MARCUS GARVEY

Words set things in motion. I've seen them doing it. Words set up atmospheres, electrical fields, charges.

TONI CADE BAMBARA

The wisdom of this year is the folly of the next.

YORUBA

Words form a hard knot that never rots.

KRU

For, while the tale of how we suffer, and how we are delighted, and how we may triumph is never new, it always must be heard. There isn't any other tale to tell, it's the only light we've got in all this darkness.

JAMES BALDWIN

There is no agony like learning an untold story inside you.

ZORA NEALE HURSTON

Ancient things remain in the ears.

OJI

Memory reaches further than the eyes.

KANURI

History, lived, not written, is such a thing not to understand always, but to marvel over. Time is so forever that life has many instances when you can say "Once upon a time" thousands of times in one life.

J. CALIFORNIA COOPER

Never give up what you have seen for what you have heard.

SWAHILI

Once our people are taught about the glorious civilization that existed on the African continent, they won't any longer be ashamed of who they are. We will reach the feeling of dignity come into us; we will make that feeling as we lived in times gone by, we can in like manner today. If we had civilizations, cultures, societies, and nations hundreds of years ago ... we can have the same today.

MALCOLM X

They call Time a old man. But Time don't age, ain't old. Every day is new. Don't nothin' age but us and what we make ... Time and Life. Well ... Time takes care of everything ... and it will take care of you.

J. CALIFORNIA COOPER

A good conversation is better than a good bed.

GALLA

Talk is the ear's food.

JAMAICA

Big word no tear man's jawbone.

JAMAICA

He who gives you the diameter of your

knowledge, prescribes the circumference of your activities.

MINISTER LOUIS FARRAKHAN

The sight of books removes sorrows from the heart.

MOROCCO

We are a people massaged by fictions; we grow up in a sea of narratives and myths, the perpetual invention of stories. When I was growing up, you sat with your age mates in the evenings and the elders would come out and tell you stories, if you asked them, or your mother would tell you stories to illustrate a hundred different points, lessons, morals, she wanted to get across to you. Or you'd tell stories more intoxicating, more beautiful. You invented stories; you were encouraged to take existing stories and weave your own variation of them.

BEN OKRI

There's a world of difference between truth and facts. Facts can obscure the truth.

MAYA ANGELOU

That which is written is binding, but that which is spoken is forgotten.

AMHARIC

The poison of a word is a word.

SWAHILI

I learned a history not then written in books but one passed from generation to generation on the steps of moonlit porches and beside dying fires in one-room houses, a history of great-grandparents and of slavery and of the days following slavery; of those who lived still not free, yet who would not let their spirits be enslaved.

MILDRED D. TAYLOR

The ear is nothing more than a door.

SURINAM

When the occasion comes the proverb comes.

OJI (ASHANTI)

Proverbs are the palm-oil with which words are eaten.

IBO

Sometimes a person has to go back, really back — to have sense, an understanding of all that's gone to make them — before they can go forward.

PAULE MARSHALL

Suddenly, it has become popular to defend tribal

people, their world view and their life ways. But while the West is engaged in a great debate about what it means to preserve culture, the indigenous world is aware that it has already lost the battle. It seems obvious to me that as soon as one culture begins to talk about "preservation" it means that it has already turned the other culture into an endangered species.

MALIDOMA PATRICE SOMÉ

A child that has never been in a strange town thinks her mother cooks best.

HO (EWE)

Talk some, leave some.

JAMAICA

The breaking day has wisdom, the falling day, experience.

NDANGA

Hour may break what age never mend.

JAMAICA

"What became of the black people of Sumer?" the traveler asked the old man, "for ancient records show that the people of Sumer were black. What happened to them?" "Ah," the old man sighed. "They lost their history, so they died."

SUMER

Why is it that the modern world can't deal with its ancestors and endure its past? It is my belief that the present state of restlessness that traps the modern individual has its roots in a dysfunctional relationship with the ancestors. In many non-Western cultures the ancestors have an intimate and absolutely vital connection with the world of the living. They are always available to guide, to teach, and to nurture. They represent one of the pathways between the knowledge of this world and the next. Most importantly, and paradoxically, of course, they embody the guidelines for successful living, all that is most valuable about life. Unless the relationship between the living and the dead is in balance, chaos results.

MALIDOMA PATRICE SOMÉ

People are easier to kill if they come from nowhere. If they have no names, no fathers or mothers. . . . The dead piles of corpses are nobodies who began nowhere, go nowhere, except back where they belong. Nowhere. No-count. Nothing.

JOHN EDGAR WIDEMAN

All is never said.

Ho

9

What You Give
Is What You Get

FORTUNE, PLENTY, PROSPERITY

If my cup won't hold but a pint, and yours holds a quart, wouldn't you be mean not to let me have my little half-measure full?

SOJOURNER TRUTH

Cow no know he lose his tail till cow-fly season.

GUYANA

A borrowed cloak doesn't keep one warm.

EGYPT

Do not borrow off the world, for the world will require its own back with interest.

SWAHILI

What a person possesses is not stronger than him or herself.

KANURI

What I have here is a complete indictment of our present day society, our whole world. What's wrong with it is money honey, money.

MARGARET WALKER

You can live without anything you weren't born with, and you can make it through on even half of that.

GLORIA NAYLOR

Work doesn't hurt — it's the eyes that are cowards.

CREOLE

Always be smarter than the people who hire you.

LENA HORNE

There is something about poverty that smells like death. Dead dreams dropping off the heart like leaves in a dry season and rotting around the feet; impulses smothered too long in the fetid air of underground caves.

ZORA NEALE HURSTON

It is work that puts one man ahead of another.

NUPE

The cultivator is one; the eaters are many.

SWAHILI

The man in debt is a swimmer with his boots on.

UNITED STATES

When a poor man makes a proverb it does not spread abroad.

OJI

Poor people entertain with the heart.

HAITIAN

The monkey says there is nothing like poverty for taking the conceit out of a man.

OJI

If one is lucky, a solitary fantasy can totally transform one million realities.

MAYA ANGELOU

People ought to do what they want to do, what else are they alive for?

JAMES BALDWIN

Your luck ain't always equal to the length of your fishing pole.

UNITED STATES

He who travels with gold shoes may reach the world's end.

AHMARIC

It is not only giants that do great things.

JABO

The work, once completed, does not need me. The work I'm working on needs my total concentration. The one that's finished doesn't belong to me anymore. It belongs to itself.

MAYA ANGELOU

Work is good provided you do not forget to live.

BANTU

The grumbler does not leave his job, but he discourages possible applicants.

GANDA

Accomplishments have no color.

LEONTYNE PRICE

If there is no struggle there is no progress.

FREDERICK DOUGLASS

If you eat egg you must break shell.

JAMAICA

A patient man has all the wealth in the world.

JABO

A roaring lion kills no game.

LANGO

You make your bed soft, you lay down soft; you

make your bed hard, you lay down hard.

WEST INDIAN

You want all, you lose all.

JAMAICA

Wealth is like hair in the nose; if much is pulled out, it is painful, if little, it is painful.

MADAGASCAR

The man that always takes the shortest road to a dollar generally takes the longest from it.

UNITED STATES

The want of a thing is more than its worth.

JAMAICA

Where there is more than enough, more than enough is wasted.

BANTU

If a child washed his hands he could eat with kings.

NIGERIA

Those whose palm kernels were cracked for them by a benevolent spirit should not forget to be humble.

CHINUA ACHEBE

Those who inherit fortunes are often more

troublesome than those who make them.

KONGO

Those who wear pearls do not know how often the shark bites the leg of the diver.

AHMARIC

The man ahead does not drink the fouled water.

BONDEI

The man who is not hungry says the coconut has a hard shell.

AHMARIC

Any old pole will find a hole in the fence.

IBO

Wealth is bits of roasted meat. The great thing is one's kith and kin.

TSONGA

A rich person is seldom condemned, for the mouth which eats another's property is benumbed.

IBO

He who has eaten doesn't make a fire for the hungry.

BASA

It is not the destiny of black America to repeat

white America's mistakes. But we will, if we mistake the trapping of success in a sick society for the signs of a meaningful life.

AUDRE LORDE

Wealth, if you use it, comes to an end; learning, if you use it, increases.

SWAHILI

If a rich man asks for children, dollars come to him, and if a poor man asks for dollars, children come to him.

MOROCCO

Everything will satisfy you except money; as much as you have, so much you want.

MOROCCO

To give away is to make provision for the future.

SOTHO

I don't sow ground nuts when the monkey is watching.

TIV (MUNSHI)

A full stomach is a snare, you go on and are in want.

TUMBULCA

The seed waits for the garden where it will be sown.

ZULU

Save money, money save you.

JAMAICA

The one-eyed man doesn't thank God till he sees the blind man.

TOUCOULEUR

Everybody to his or her own calling and none to any other.

BAKONGO

It was his firm conviction that Allah left the question of a means of livelihood for each man to decide for himself. Allah, he was sure, gives some people more than they need so that others with too little could help themselves to some of it.

DAVID OWOYELE

10

On the Ladder Universal

POLITICS, POWER, JUSTICE

As a leader . . . I have always endeavored to listen to what each and every person in a discussion had to say before venturing my own opinion. Oftentimes, my own opinion will simply represent a consensus of what I heard in the discussion. I always remember the . . . axiom: a leader . . . is like a shepherd. He stays behind the flock, letting the most nimble go out ahead, whereupon the others follow, not realizing that all along they are being directed from behind.

NELSON MANDELA

When you go to a country where they all dance with one foot, then dance with one foot, too.

CARIBBEAN

Hope is the pillar of the world.

KANURI

One hand can't tie a bundle.

BASA

If everybody start this business of dreamin', makin' a special little kind of world of dreams for themselves there won't be no need for what they call the politics. They won't have much time to think 'bout anything that concern a lot o' people put together at the same said time. An' when everybody get that feeling for himself then there won't be no more the people. 'Twill only be me an' you an' he an' she.

GEORGE LAMMING

We are people because of other people.

SOTHO

Unity among the cattle makes the lion lie down hungry.

SWAHILI

Once a baboon has tasted honey it does not touch earth again.

TSONGA

If a bee didn't have sting, him would no keep him honey.

JAMAICA

Cross the river before you abuse the crocodile.

FANTI

Power never takes a back step — only in the face of more power. . . . Power recognizes only power, and all of them who realize this have made gains.

MALCOLM X

It's . . . important for people who think alike, both black and white, to form a united front against the government, so that the fight will not be black against white but right against wrong.

LEWIS NKOSI

We are all bound up together in one great bundle of humanity, and society cannot trample on the weakest and feeblest of its members without receiving the curse in its own soul.

FRANCES ELLEN WATKINS

If you're going to hold someone down you're going to have to hold onto the other and of the chain. You are confined by your own system of repression.

TONI MORRISON

Respect depends on reciprocity.

NYANG

Sometimes, I feel discriminated against, but it does not make me angry. It merely astonishes me. How can any deny themselves the pleasure of my company? It's beyond me.

ZORA NEALE HURSTON

Equality in injustice is justice.

EGYPT

The bones before being thrown into the street were on the master's table.

SURINAM

I beg of you to remember that whenever our life touches yours we help or hinder ... whenever your life touches ours, you make us stronger or weaker. ... There is no escape — man drags man down, or man lifts man up.

BOOKER T. WASHINGTON

To move beyond the victim-focused black identity we must learn to make a difficult but crucial distinction: between actual victimization, which we must resist with every resource, and identification with the victim's status. Until we do this we will continue to wrestle more with ourselves than with the new opportunities so many paid so dearly to win.

SHELBY STEELE

Cockroaches never get justice when chicken judges.

JAMAICA

As you grow older ... you must learn that men are punished not always for what they do, but often for what people think they will do, or for what they are. Remember that and you will find it easier to forgive them.

NICO ABIOSEH

I knew as well as I knew anything that the oppressor must be liberated just as surely as the oppressed. A man who takes away another man's freedom is a prisoner of hatred, he is locked behind the bars of prejudice and narrow-mindedness. I am not truly free if I am taking away someone else's freedom, just as surely as I am not free when my freedom is taken from me. The oppressed and the oppressor alike are robbed of freedom.

NELSON MANDELA

Justice becomes injustice when it makes two wounds on a head which only deserves one.

BAKONGO

The price of liberation of the white people is the liberation of the blacks — the total liberation, in the cities, in the towns, before the law, and in the mind.

JAMES BALDWIN

The black man who cannot let love and sympathy go out to the white man is but half free. The white man who retards his own development by opposing the black man is but half free.

BOOKER T. WASHINGTON

The chief is like a rubbish heap; everything comes to him.

NGONE

The chief has no relative.

TSONGA

There is little place in the political scheme of things for an independent, creative personality, for a fighter. Anyone who takes that role must pay the price.

SHIRLEY CHISHOLM

A man who creates trouble seldom eats it himself.

BANTU

A devotion to humanity . . . is too easily equated with a devotion to a cause, and causes, as we know, are notoriously bloodthirsty.

JAMES BALDWIN

Nothing in the world is more dangerous than a sincere ignorance and conscientious stupidity.

MARTIN LUTHER KING, JR.

Power recognizes only power, and all of them who realize this have made gains.

MALCOLM X

> Independence is we nature
> Born and bred in all we do,
> And we glad fe see dat government
> Turn independent too.
>
> JAMAICA

No one can understand the action of Mrs. Parks unless he realizes that eventually the cup of endurance runs over, and the human personality cries out, "I can take it no longer." Mrs. Park's refusal to move [to the back of the bus] was her intrepid affirmation that she had had enough. It was an individual expression of a timeless longing for human dignity and freedom ... she was anchored to that seat by the accumulated indignities of days gone by and the boundless aspirations of generations yet unborn. She was a victim of both the sources of history and the forces of destiny. She had been tracked down by the Zeitgeist — the spirit of the time.

MARTIN LUTHER KING, JR.

It took the colored people a long time to realize that . . . to be a citizen of the United States was serious business, and a seat in Congress was an insecure prominence unless supported by good women, noble mothers, family integrity, and fine homes.

FANNIE BARRIER WILLIAMS

If they come for me in the morning, they will come for you at night.

ANGELA DAVIS

Education is the great engine of personal development. It is through education that the daughter of a peasant can become a doctor, that the son of a mine worker can become the head of the mine, that a child of farmworkers can become the president of a great nation. It is what we make out of what we have, not what we are given, that separates one person from another.

NELSON MANDELA

We decide our affairs, then rest them with God.

JABO

I have walked that long road to freedom . . . but I have discovered the secret that after climbing a great hill, one only finds that there are many more hills to climb. I have taken a moment here to rest, to steal a view of the glorious vista that surrounds me, to look back on the distance I have come. But I can rest only for a moment, for with freedom comes responsibilities, and I dare not linger, for my long walk is not ended.

NELSON MANDELA

If God be for us who can be against us?

DESMOND TUTU

11

The Eternal Spirit
Is the Only Reality

SPIRIT, NATURE, GOD, FAITH

Powerful One, I know thee as the first
man.
Even in the dark I can see thou art
powerful.
In the whole world nothing is hidden
from thee.

TRADITIONAL CANDOMBLE SONG, BRAZIL

In Eastern philosophies we see ourselves as a part of a life force; we are joined, for instance, to the air, to the earth. We are part of the whole-life process. We live in accordance with, in a kind of correspondence with the rest of the world as a whole. And therefore living becomes an experience, rather than a problem, no matter how bad or painful it may be.

AUDRE LORDE

A man who doesn't believe in miracles may come to believe in them tomorrow. Proofs occur every day, some more convincing than others, but all quite reasonable.

ESTEBAN MONTEJO

I'll bet when you get down on them rusty knees and get to worrying God, He just goes in his privy house and slams the door. That's what he thinking about you and your prayers.

ZORA NEALE HURSTON

I had assumed that the Earth, the spirit of the Earth, noticed exceptions — those who wantonly damage it and those who do not. But the earth is wise. It has given itself into the keeping of all, and all are therefore accountable.

UNITED STATES

"The sea ain't got no back door" ... meaning that it wasn't like a house where if there was a fire you could run out the back. Meaning that it was not to be trifled with. And meaning perhaps in a larger sense that man should treat all of nature with caution and respect.

PAULE MARSHALL

As for God ... God ... don' love ugly and He ain't stuck on pretty.

PAULE MARSHALL

Slowness comes from God and quickness from devil.

MOROCCO

Healing without medicine is a good thing.

MADAGASCAR

To commit ten sins against God is better than to commit one sin against a servant of God.

MOROCCO

Our society allows people to be absolutely neurotic and totally out of touch with their feelings, and yet be very respectable.

NTOZAKE SHANGE

A tree is very important to a Congolese, because everything comes from it and is to be found in it. It is like a god; they feed it and talk to it and ask things of it and look after it. Everything they do is with the help of Nature, especially the tree, which is the soul of Nature.

ESTEBAN MONTEJO

God gives and does not remind us continually of it; the world gives and constantly reminds us.

NUPE

The wilderness has ears.

KAMBA

Water is the king of food.

KANURI

To imagine something, to closely focus one's thoughts upon it, has the potential to bring that "something" into being. Thus, people who take a tragic view of life and are always expecting the worst, usually manifest that reality. Those who expect that things will work together for the good, usually experience just that. In the realm of the sacred, this concept is taken even further, for what is magic but the ability to focus thought and energy to get results on the human plane. My people's view of reality is large. If one can imagine something, it has, at least, the potential to exist.

MALIDOMA PATRICE SOMÉ

Leave the battle to God and rest your head upon your hand.

YORUBA

When the person who has inherited his father's god prays to it that he may neither die nor suffer illness, the question might be asked, "What became of the person who first introduced the worship of the god into the family?"

YORUBA

The best passion is *com*passion.

JAMAICA

Prayer needn't be long when faith is strong.

JAMAICA

It is not our custom to fight for our gods. . . . Let us not presume to do so now. If a man kills the sacred python in the secrecy of his hut, the matter is between him and the god. We did not see it. If we put ourselves between the god and his victim we may receive blows intended for the offender. When a man blasphemes, what do we do? Do we go and stop his mouth? No, we put our fingers into our ears to stop us hearing. That is a wise action.

CHINUA ACHEBE

There are things about life I don't understand. Everything about Nature is obscure to me, and about the gods more so still. The gods are capricious and willful, and they are the cause of many strange things which can happen here and which I have seen for myself. I can remember as a slave I spent half my time gazing up at the sky because it looked so painted. Once it suddenly turned the color of hot coal, and there was a terrible drought. Another time was an eclipse of the sun which started at four in the afternoon and could be seen all over the island. I noticed that everything seemed to be going backwards — it got darker and darker, and then lighter and lighter. Hens flew up to roost. People were too frightened to speak. Some died of heart failure and others were struck dumb.

ESTEBAN MONTEJO

The Bible is the white man's tool ... when the white man came to these shores, he had the Bibles and the blacks had the land. Now he has the land and they have the Bibles.

FARIDA KARODIA

Follow the holy man no farther than his threshold.

EGYPT

Listen, God love everything you love — and a mess of stuff you don't. But more than anything else, God love admiration.... I think it pisses God off if you walk by the color purple in a field somewhere and don't notice it.

ALICE WALKER

Nothing that God ever made is the same thing

to more than one person.

ZORA NEALE HURSTON

Don't blame God for having created the tiger, but give him thanks for not having given the tiger wings.

AMHARIC

The man who goes to the spirit world has no bribe or ordeal.

BONDEI

Children talk with God.

BATSWANA

Every knot has an unraveller in God.

EGYPT

God provides even for the insect between two stones.

EGYPT

The woods, tall as waves, sang in mixed tongues that loosened the scalp.

SONIA SANCHEZ

Every day we get closer to living in a global community. With distances between culture narrowing, we have much wisdom to gain by learning to understand other people's cultures and permitting ourselves to accept that there is more than one version of reality. To exist in the first place, each culture has to have its own version of what is real. . . . In the culture of my people . . . we have no word for the supernatural. . . . In Western reality there is a clear split between the spiritual and the material, between the religious life and secular life . . . but for many indigenous cultures, the supernatural is part of our everyday lives. To us the material is just the spiritual taking on form. The secular is religion in a lower key, a rest area from the tension of religious and spiritual practice.

MALIDOMA PATRICE SOMÉ

If you are going to ask from God, take a big receptacle.

HAUSA

About the Editor

Winner of the O. Henry Award, the Whiting Writer's Award, and two-time winner of the Kenyon Review Award for Literary Excellence for the story "The Kind of Light That Shines on Texas," and "The More I Like Flies," Reginald McKnight holds many such awards among his list of accomplishments. McKnight is the recipient of a Thomas J. Watson Foundation Fellowship and a 1991 National Endowment for the Arts Grant for Literature. His first collection of short stories, *Moustapha's Eclipse*, was awarded the 1988 Drue Heinz Literature Prize.

McKnight is also the author of the critically acclaimed novel *I Get On the Bus*, the short story collection *The Kind of Light That Shines on Texas*, and the Classic Wisdom bestseller *African American Wisdom*. He is a professor of English at the University of Maryland and lives in Baltimore, Maryland.

Bibliographical Index

The information in this index allows the reader to locate the contributors and authors within the text and to further explore their writing. Applicable publisher permissions follow the index.

phasizes the paradoxical nature of the African woman's role today. *Dilemma of a Ghost* (1964); *Our Sister Killjoy, or, Reflections of a Black-eyed Squint* (1966); *No Sweetness Here* (1970), 76

Amoja Three Rivers, A Pittsburg Black Cultural Arts Group, 27, 28

Anderson, Ernestine (1928-) American jazz, blues singer, 60

Anderson, Marian (1902-) Opera singer, one of the finest contraltos of her time. Ulrica in Verdi's "A Masked Ball" *(My Lord, What a Morning [autobiography] 1957)*, 69

Angelou, Maya (1928-) Actress, singer, educator, activist, poet; Reynolds Professor at Wake Forrest University; U.S. Poet Laureate, *Just Give Me a Cool Drink of Water 'For I Die; And Still I Rise; Wouldn't Take Nothing for My Fourney Now; I Know Why the Caged Bird Sings* (autobiography, 1970), 37, 47, 56, 95, 101, 102

Armah, Ayi Kwei (1939-) Ghanaian-born writer, now living in Dakar, Senegal; *The Beautiful Ones Are Not Yet Born* (1968); *Fragments* (1970); *Why Are We So Blest?* (1972); *Two Thousand Seasons* (1973); *The Healers* (1978), 63

Awoonor, Kofi (Formerly George Awoonor Williams 1935-) Ghanaian poet, novelist, and critic. Awarded the 1988 Commonwealth Poetry Prize for the African area for *Until the Morning After: Collected Poems* (1987); *This Earth, My Brother ... An*

documentarist, information officer for the Nigerian Government (1960-61), 99

Clark, Septima Poinsette (1898-1987) Civil rights activist. Suffragist, known as "queen mother" of the civil rights movement, 61

Clifton, Lucille Sayles (1936-) U.S.-born poet and children's story writer; *The Boy Who Didn't Believe in Spring* (1973); *Everett Anderson's Christmas Coming* (1991); *Good Woman: Poems and a Memoir 1969-80* (1987), 60

Cooper, California J. (20th c.) American; author of *A Piece of Mine*; *Homemade Love*; *Some Soul to Keep and Family* (1991), 55, 93, 94

Cooper, Julia Anna (19th c.) U.S. educator, suffragist, orator and writer of *Voice of the South* (1892), 52

Davis, Angela (Yvonne) (1944-) Highly public political activist in 1960s and 1970s, highly acclaimed professor of philosophy, aesthetics and women's studies at San Francisco State University and the San Francisco Art Institute *(Angela Davis: An Autobiography*, 1988; *Women, Race and Class*, 1982), 114

Davis, Ossie (1917-) Actor, author of *Escape to Freedom* (1990), 61

Dee, Ruby (20th c.) Actor, author, poet, 36, 51

Diop, Birago (20th c.) Senegal writer, *Tales of Amadow Koumba* (1966), 89

Douglass, Frederick (1817-1895) An escaped slave whose brilliance as an orator, writer, and journalist

ist, critic, writer; *Meridian* (1976); *The Third Life of Grange Copeland* (1970); Winner of the Pulitzer Prize for *The Color Purple* in 1983; *The Temple of My Familiar* (1989); *Possessing the Secret of Joy* (1993), 52, 61, 84, 122

Walker, Margaret Alexander (1915-) Poet, essayist, novelist, educator; Emeritus professor of English at Jackson State University in Mississippi; *For My People* (1942); *Jubilee* (1966), 100

Washington, Booker T. (Taliaferro) (1856-1915) American educator and reformer; first president and principal developer of Tuskeegee Institute, advisor to presidents Theodore Roosevelt and William Howard Taft on racial matters, and the most influential spokesperson for black Americans from 1895-1915. Author of *Up from Slavery* (autobiography, 1901), 110, 112

Watkins, Frances Ellen (1825-1911) Abolitionist, social activist, poet, 109

Weems, Renita J. (20th c.) American writer, educator, member of clergy; *I Asked for Intimacy: Stories of Blessing, Betrayals, Birthings* (1993); *Just a Sister Away: A Womanist Vision of Women's Relationships in the Bible* (1988), 48

Wideman, John Edgar (1941-) Novelist *(Sent for You Yesterday*, 1983; *Fever*, 1989), winner of the 1984 PEN/Faulkner Award, 26, 53, 98

Williams, Chancellor (20th c.) U.S. Historian educator,

Permissions

Grateful acknowledgment is made to the following for permission to reprint excerpts from previously published and unpublished material:

CLEVELAND STATE UNIVERSITY PRESS, Cleveland, OH. *Hurdy-Gurdy* © 1992 by Tim Seibles.

UNPUBLISHED. *Marvin Loves — If This World Were Mine* © by Jonathon Smith.

The Classic Wisdom Collection

If you would like a catalog of our fine
books and cassettes, contact:

NEW WORLD LIBRARY
14 Pamaron Way
Novato, California 94949
(415) 884-2100
FAX (415) 884-2199

Or call toll-free: (800) 227-3900